# Francis Frith's
# Around York

*Photographic Memories*

# Francis Frith's
# Around York

Maureen Anderson

FRITH
BOOK Co

Paperback edition published in the United Kingdom in 2000 by
Frith Book Company Ltd
ISBN 1-85937-199-x

Hardback reprinted in 2000
ISBN 1-85937-296-1

British Library Cataloguing in Publication Data

Francis Frith's Around York
Maureen Anderson

Frith Book Company Ltd
Frith's Barn, Teffont,
Salisbury, Wiltshire SP3 5QP
Tel: +44 (0) 1722 716 376
Email: info@frithbook.co.uk
www.frithbook.co.uk


Printed and bound in Great Britain

*Front Cover:* Coney Street 1909  61723

AS WITH ANY HISTORICAL DATABASE THE FRITH ARCHIVE IS CONSTANTLY BEING CORRECTED AND IMPROVED
AND THE PUBLISHERS WOULD WELCOME INFORMATION ON OMISSIONS OR INACCURACIES

# Contents

# Francis Frith: *Victorian Pioneer*

**FRANCIS FRITH**, Victorian founder of the world-famous photographic archive, was a complex and multi-talented man. A devout Quaker and a highly successful Victorian businessman, he was both philosophic by nature and pioneering in outlook.

By 1855 Francis Frith had already established a wholesale grocery business in Liverpool, and sold it for the astonishing sum of £200,000, which is the equivalent today of over £15,000,000. Now a multi-millionaire, he was able to indulge his passion for travel. As a child he had pored over travel books written by early explorers, and his fancy and imagination had been stirred by family holidays to the sublime mountain regions of Wales and Scotland. 'What a land of spirit-stirring and enriching scenes and places!' he had written. He was to return to these scenes of grandeur in later years to 'recapture the thousands of vivid and tender memories', but with a different purpose. Now in his thirties, and captivated by the new science of photography, Frith set out on a series of

pioneering journeys to the Nile regions that occupied him from 1856 until 1860.

## Intrigue and Adventure

He took with him on his travels a specially-designed wicker carriage that acted as both dark-room and sleeping chamber. These far-flung journeys were packed with intrigue and adventure. In his life story, written when he was sixty-three, Frith tells of being held captive by bandits, and of fighting 'an awful midnight battle to the very point of surrender with a deadly pack of hungry, wild dogs'. Sporting flowing Arab costume, Frith arrived at Akaba by camel seventy years before Lawrence, where he encountered 'desert princes and rival sheikhs, blazing with jewel-hilted swords'.

During these extraordinary adventures he was assiduously exploring the desert regions bordering the Nile and patiently recording the antiquities and peoples with his camera. He was the first photographer to venture beyond the sixth cataract. Africa was still the mysterious 'Dark Continent', and Stanley and Livingstone's historic meeting was a decade into the future. The conditions for picture taking confound belief. He laboured for hours in his wicker dark-room in the sweltering heat of the desert, while the volatile chemicals fizzed dangerously in their trays. Often he was forced to work in remote tombs and caves where conditions were cooler. Back in London he exhibited his photographs and was 'rapturously cheered' by members of the Royal Society. His reputation as a photographer was made overnight. An eminent modern historian has likened their impact on the population of the time to that on our own generation of the first photographs taken on the surface of the moon.

## Venture of a Life-Time

Characteristically, Frith quickly spotted the opportunity to create a new business as a specialist publisher of photographs. He lived in an era of immense and sometimes violent change. For the poor in the early part of Victoria's reign work was a drudge and the hours long, and people had precious little free time to enjoy themselves. Most had no transport other than a cart or gig at their disposal, and had not travelled far beyond the

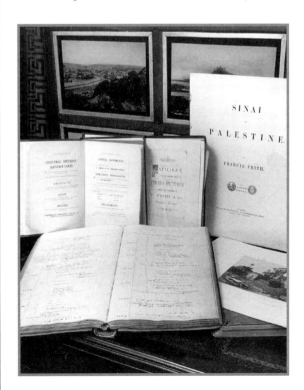

boundaries of their own town or village. However, by the 1870s, the railways had threaded their way across the country, and Bank Holidays and half-day Saturdays had been made obligatory by Act of Parliament. All of a sudden the ordinary working man and his family were able to enjoy days out and see a little more of the world.

With characteristic business acumen, Francis Frith foresaw that these new tourists would enjoy having souvenirs to commemorate their days out. In 1860 he married Mary Ann Rosling and set out with the intention of photographing every city, town and village in Britain. For the next thirty years he travelled the country by train and by pony and trap, producing fine photographs of seaside resorts and beauty spots that were keenly bought by millions of Victorians. These prints were painstakingly pasted into family albums and pored over during the dark nights of winter, rekindling precious memories of summer excursions.

## The Rise of Frith & Co

Frith's studio was soon supplying retail shops all over the country. To meet the demand he gathered about him a small team of photographers, and published the work of independent artist-photographers of the calibre of Roger Fenton and Francis Bedford. In order to gain some understanding of the scale of Frith's business one only has to look at the catalogue issued by Frith & Co in 1886: it runs to some 670 pages, listing not only many thousands of views of the British Isles but also many photographs of most European countries, and China, Japan, the USA and

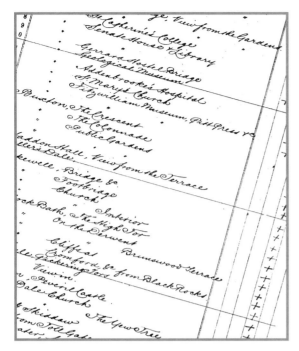

Canada – note the sample page shown above from the hand-written *Frith & Co* ledgers detailing pictures taken. By 1890 Frith had created the greatest specialist photographic publishing company in the world, with over 2,000 outlets – more than the combined number that Boots and WH Smith have today! The picture on the right shows the *Frith & Co* display board at Ingleton in the Yorkshire Dales. Beautifully constructed with mahogany frame and gilt inserts, it could display up to a dozen local scenes.

## Postcard Bonanza

The ever-popular holiday postcard we know today took many years to develop. In 1870 the Post Office issued the first plain cards, with a pre-printed stamp on one face. In 1894 they allowed other publishers' cards to be sent through the mail with an attached adhesive halfpenny stamp. Demand grew rapidly, and in 1895 a new size of postcard was permitted called the court card, but there was little room for illustration. In 1899, a year after Frith's death, a new card measuring 5.5 x 3.5 inches became the standard format, but it was not until 1902 that the divided back came into being, with address and message on one face and a full-size illustration on the other. *Frith & Co* were in the vanguard of postcard development, and Frith's sons Eustace and Cyril continued their father's monumental task, expanding the number of views offered to the public and recording more and more places in Britain, as the coasts and countryside were opened up to mass travel.

Francis Frith died in 1898 at his villa in Cannes, his great project still growing. The archive he created continued in business for another seventy years. By 1970 it contained over a third of a million pictures of 7,000 cities, towns and villages. The massive photographic record Frith has left to us stands as a living monument to a special and very remarkable man.

# Frith's Archive: *A Unique Legacy*

**FRANCIS FRITH'S** legacy to us today is of immense significance and value, for the magnificent archive of evocative photographs he created provides a unique record of change in 7,000 cities, towns and villages throughout Britain over a century and more. Frith and his fellow studio photographers revisited locations many times down the years to update their views, compiling for us an enthralling and colourful pageant of British life and character.

We tend to think of Frith's sepia views of Britain as nostalgic, for most of us use them to conjure up memories of places in our own lives with which we have family associations. It often makes us forget that to Francis Frith they were records of daily life as it was actually being lived in the cities, towns and villages of his day. The Victorian age was one of great and often bewildering change for ordinary people, and though the pictures evoke an impression of slower times, life was as busy and hectic as it is today.

We are fortunate that Frith was a photographer of the people, dedicated to recording the minutiae of everyday life. For it is this sheer wealth of visual data, the painstaking chronicle of changes in dress, transport, street layouts, buildings, housing, engineering and landscape that captivates us so much today. His remarkable images offer us a powerful link with the past and with the lives of our ancestors.

## Today's Technology

Computers have now made it possible for Frith's many thousands of images to be accessed almost instantly. In the Frith archive today, each photograph is carefully 'digitised' then stored on a CD Rom. Frith archivists can locate a single photograph amongst thousands within seconds. Views can be catalogued and sorted under a variety of categories of place and content to the immediate benefit of researchers.

Inexpensive reference prints can be created for them at the touch of a mouse button, and a wide range of books and other printed materials assembled and published for a wider, more general readership - in the next twelve months over a hundred Frith local history titles will be published! The day-to-day workings of the archive are very different from how they were in Francis Frith's time: imagine the herculean task of sorting through eleven tons of glass negatives as Frith had to do to locate a particular

**See Frith at www. frithbook.co.uk**

sequence of pictures! Yet the archive still prides itself on maintaining the same high standards of excellence laid down by Francis Frith, including the painstaking cataloguing and indexing of every view.

It is curious to reflect on how the internet now allows researchers in America and elsewhere greater instant access to the archive than Frith himself ever enjoyed. Many thousands of individual views can be called up on screen within seconds on one of the Frith internet sites, enabling people living continents away to revisit the streets of their ancestral home town, or view places in Britain where they have enjoyed holidays. Many overseas researchers welcome the chance to view special theme selections, such as transport, sports, costume and ancient monuments.

We are certain that Francis Frith would have heartily approved of these modern developments in imaging techniques, for he himself was always working at the very limits of Victorian photographic technology.

## The Value of the Archive Today

Because of the benefits brought by the computer, Frith's images are increasingly studied by social historians, by researchers into genealogy and ancestry, by architects, town planners, and by teachers and schoolchildren involved in local history projects.

In addition, the archive offers every one of us an opportunity to examine the places where we and our families have lived and worked down the years. Highly successful in Frith's own era, the archive is now, a century and more on, entering a new phase of popularity.

## The Past in Tune with the Future

Historians consider the Francis Frith Collection to be of prime national importance. It is the only archive of its kind remaining in private ownership and has been valued at a million pounds. However, this figure is now rapidly increasing as digital technology enables more and more people around the world to enjoy its benefits.

Francis Frith's archive is now housed in an historic timber barn in the beautiful village of Teffont in Wiltshire. Its founder would not recognize the archive office as it is today. In place of the many thousands of dusty boxes containing glass plate negatives and an all-pervading odour of photographic chemicals, there are now ranks of computer screens. He would be amazed to watch his images travelling round the world at unimaginable speeds through network and internet lines.

The archive's future is both bright and exciting. Francis Frith, with his unshakeable belief in making photographs available to the greatest number of people, would undoubtedly approve of what is being done today with his lifetime's work. His photographs, depicting our shared past, are now bringing pleasure and enlightenment to millions around the world a century and more after his death.

# York - *An Introduction*

YORK IS JUST less than 220 miles from London, and is located within the boundaries of North Yorkshire in the beautiful Vale of York. The population is 177,350 - a portion of this is made up of the student body that attend the relatively new university. Much of the surrounding area is still very much agricultural; a substantial amount of the economy derives from the food industry as well as from tourism. Once an encampment, and originally built at the confluence of the River Ouse and the River Foss, the city now spans a much wider area on both sides of the two rivers. Until the Industrial Revolution, which largely passed it by, York was once the most important town in the north of England.

In Roman times, York was the principal military base in Britain, and in the 9th century it was the capital of a Viking kingdom. Because of its importance in the scheme of things, some records have survived; these records, along with what has been excavated, have enabled historians and archaeologists to piece together a vast amount of York's past. Its rich history spans more than nineteen centuries. York began in 71 AD as a Roman camp, which was home to some 6,000 soldiers. The Romans named the outpost Eboracum, which is thought to have meant 'a place of yew trees'. The location would have been chosen because the rivers would help protect it from attack; ironically, centuries later, the Vikings used the rivers as their gateway for invasion. Near the soldiers' encampment a civilian town sprang up, which was peopled by the traders and their families who supplied the soldiers with clothing, food and the things necessary to life. One Roman building that still stands is the Multiangular Tower; there is also a column that stands 30 feet high which was found during excavations to the

Minster in 1969, lying where it had fallen. The York Civic Trust had it erected in the Minster Yard in 1971. A public house called the Roman Bath Inn has a floor made up of panels of glass where one can look onto the remains of a Roman bath house that was excavated in 1930.

During the Saxon period, Eboracum became known as Eoforwic. This period is the least documented, but we do know that the Saxons were instrumental in the spread of Christianity and established the foundations for many of the churches. In 866 the Vikings invaded, and changed the name of the town to Jorvik. Some of the place names, such as Micklegate and Goodramgate, are inheritances from the occupation, although the Vikings were here for less than a century. As with the Romans, not many of the buildings above ground have survived, but excavations have turned up many well-preserved artefacts. The Jorvik Viking Centre, a huge tourist attraction which brings millions of visitors every year, is built upon the site of an excavated Viking settlement, and the artefacts found here have been used in the museum. Even the Viking rubbish dumps were a treasure trove to the historians: shoes, utensils and bits of clothing that had been discarded all serve to show the Viking way of life. The impression we have formed of these people is of frightening-looking men with huge beards and horned helmets who spent their lives burning, raping and pillaging; but the excavations of their settlements show a different picture. The Jorvik Centre proves that once the Vikings put down roots in an area, they had a settled family life.

During the Norman period, in 1089, a large cathedral was built; many churches were built too, some of which have survived. The 13th century saw building begin on a new cathedral replacing the earlier edifice. The building of the present Minster was spread over a period of 250 years. Recently an enormous amount of restoration work has been carried out all over York. There are approximately 1,000 listed buildings in the city, and about twenty of these are churches. The Georgians and then the Victorians have also left their legacies in many of the wonderful buildings that still remain.

The Romans had built walls spanning nearly three miles in an almost complete circuit around their encampment; chains were stretched across the rivers where they prevented the continuation of the walls. Thus the outpost became a fortress town. The Vikings covered these walls with earth. Then, in medieval times, the walls that still stand today were built on top of the original ramparts with magnesian limestone brought from Tadcaster. The four main entrance gates still survive.

Oil lamps were used until 1824, when gas lighting was introduced to the streets. How the people must have rejoiced to be able to walk the

streets in comparative brightness instead of in the murky light of the old lamps. It is said that well over a hundred ghosts can still be seen or heard in the city; the popular Ghost Walks take visitors on a tour of public houses, churches and other buildings as the sad tales behind the hauntings are told. One story is of the Towpath Ghost, a white headless lady who is said to wander up and down the Ouse towpath looking for the people who robbed and killed her while she was strolling along the riverbank. Her body lay hidden for so long that the head had separated from the body. Another story is of children crying; they were supposed to have been killed by the wicked master of a ragged school. Whether one believes in ghosts or not, in a city with such a long and sometimes quite violent history, with so many tears and so much laughter, with so many births and deaths, something must surely remain. Perhaps the spirits of the people that have lived here through the ages are impregnated into the walls and buildings.

Besides the hauntings, there are many stories of the people who made their mark on York's history, names that will never be forgotten. They include Roman soldiers and emperors, Vikings such as Eric Bloodaxe, and the dukes of York, six of whom were crowned king; more recently there was Guy Fawkes, who was born here, Dick Turpin, who spent his last days in the condemned cell of the prison, and Margaret Clitherow, who was proclaimed a saint. She was married to a butcher from the Shambles in the 16th century. Arrested for harbouring priests and refusing to plead, she was tried at what was then the Common Hall (now the Guildhall) and sentenced to death by pressing. A house in the Shambles is now set aside as a shrine to her.

Tradition still plays a key role here. At Christmas the high altar in the Minster has mistletoe placed upon it as decoration; the plant said to have magical properties and its associations are pagan, so it is unknown how this practice came to be. Displays of sword dancing are held in St Sampson's Square on Plough Monday, the first Monday after 6 January; again the origins of this custom are unknown - the dancing was once performed by farm labourers. The Mystery Plays are performed in the Minster Yard, usually by amateur groups; 'mystery' derives from the word 'mastery', and all the plays are biblical.

The pride of the city, and one of the most famous buildings in the world, is York Minster, York's cathedral, which was completed in 1472 and restored between 1967 and 1972. An enormous edifice, it boasts wonderful Gothic architecture, woodwork and stonework, and also stained glass, 128 windows in all, spanning 800 years of glass painting. One part of a medieval glass panel shows that the painter had a sense of humour - it depicts what is known as the

Monkey's Funeral. Nine monkeys are pictured: the deceased is carried shoulder-high by four pallbearers, while a bell-ringer leads the procession with a cross-bearer behind. The bereaved young monkey is in the centre foreground, being comforted by a friend. Last but not least, one monkey is sampling the wine at the funeral feast. The Minster is still used for daily worship, as well as for services on important occasions. The organ music is known world-wide. Scholars come to study the Minster's history and to use the library, and tourists flock from all over the world to wonder at its beauty.

Although the chimney stacks and the large dull grey buildings relating to heavy industry never made a serious impact on York, the sweet industry made its mark. The origins of Rowntree Mackintosh's and Terry's chocolate empires began in retail businesses in the 18th century. The businesses eventually developed into large-scale confectionery manufacture; in the late 1930s they were employing over 12,000 people. Both these firms are still major players in the confectionery and food industry today. Glass works and instrument-making were also once big business. The coming of the railway had a huge impact, and brought prosperity to many. George Hudson, dubbed 'the Railway King', was instrumental in the development of the railway and its related buildings. He was three times Lord Mayor, but eventually crooked wheeling and

dealing with funds brought his downfall; for over a century his name was shunned in York. In recent years, however, his input has been recognised, and a street and a building have been named after him.

There was a long wait for a university in this city, but once plans were approved, work went ahead quite quickly. Some older historical buildings were incorporated into the structure of the plans and the first two colleges were opened in the 1960s, with others following over the next few years.

Such is the wealth of preserved history here, that days rather than hours are needed to tour this amazing city. On turning a corner, beautiful old trees, some older than the buildings, stretch their branches to the sky where you would least expect it. The ruins of St Mary's Abbey stand in the peaceful, well-manicured Museum Gardens, giving an insight of how harsh life must have been: the thick stone walls and open fires were the only protection from the cold. There is a wealth of medieval stained glass in some of the churches and in many of the buildings, as well as in the Minster. Along the snickelways, we can look above the shop fronts and see public house signs, tea shop signs, statues, carvings, gargoyles and so on - they show what the buildings were once used for or who once lived there. As we walk along the walls, we can see breathtaking views of the rivers and the city. Many buildings that have been

preserved or painstakingly restored are open to the public; some are instantly recognisable in this compilation of photographs taken more than a century ago. At dusk many of the buildings are now floodlit. Modern gift shops and cafes now line the little streets, and millions of visitors from every corner of the world tour the city every year, but that does not take anything away from the magical atmosphere - indeed, it seems instead to enhance it. Whatever we do or see here, it gives us an unforgettable experience of a journey back in time.

Just as the tides of the rivers have ebbed and flowed unrelentingly through the ages, so has the history and prosperity of this ancient city. Although the buildings from so many different eras and of differing architectural styles are side by side, somehow they all live together in perfect harmony. They give the impression that here the past merges into the present, and also that the city of York will endure to give pleasure to future generations - and also to teach them that knowing about their heritage can help to shape the future.

# Places of Worship
# and the Gateways of the City

The present Minster is not the first place of worship to be built on the site. It is believed that there was first a wooden church, then one of stone, which were followed by three other churches. Some of these were destroyed by fire: the worst was in 1137, which not only raged through the church but also destroyed a large portion of the town, including St Mary's Abbey and another thirty-nine churches. Many of the present churches stand on the sites of older places of worship which had the same dedications and date from well before the Norman Conquest. Most of the medieval churches were supported and maintained by the parishioners, and eventually they became too costly for the communities to support. A few were owned by religious houses, so these managed to survive; but many of the smaller parishes were forced to join up with each other, and that meant that some of the churches were left to rot or were demolished. The stone from these churches was often used in other buildings.

The stained glass in York is considered to be among the finest in the world. The glass that survives in the Minster and the medieval churches was often donated in memory of someone after a bereavement, or as a gift, by wealthy families who were parishioners of that particular church.

Walmgate Bar, to the south-east, is the first of the four main gates. The house on the inner side of the bar is now a bookshop. As we follow the walls, we come to many towers and six more modest gates, or bars. A stretch of the walls near Micklegate Bar to the south-west once marked the southern boundary of Holy Trinity Priory. The lower parts of the bar were constructed before the medieval walls. The barbican here partially collapsed, and it was removed in 1826. It was similar to the one still standing at Walmgate. Many English sovereigns have passed through here, including William the Conqueror and Edward VII. Bootham Bar is on the north-east of the circuit. The barbican was removed and replaced by buttresses in about 1832. This is the only one of the four bars to have no doors on the first-floor room for access to the parapets of the barbican; it is thought, therefore, that the barbican may have been added to the gatehouse at a later time. Just past Bootham Bar we can see the best views of the Minster from the walls. Situated to the north-west, Monk Bar was once known as Monkgate. The barbican here was demolished in 1825 to make way for a footpath. Inside there are vaulted stone ceilings and bartizans, which are small circular rooms. The bar is now open to the public as an art gallery.

**The Old Rectory 1909** 61864
This was the rectory to the medieval St Denys's Church. It was demolished in 1939, and an office block now stands on the site. The church was badly damaged during the siege of York, and eventually in 1846 the spire and the west end were removed, making it about half of its original size. Some of the glass here is the oldest in York, dating from the 12th century.

**All Saints' Church, Pavement 1921** 70648

### All Saints' Church
### Pavement 1921

Standing tranquilly a few minutes away from the town centre, this church was built in the 11th century. Over time it has had many changes. The tower and spire were added in the 15th century; the spire rises to a height of 120 feet. Some of the most beautiful stained glass in England adorns the windows of the building.

### Holy Trinity Church
### Goodramgate 1909

Largely rebuilt in 1860, this was known as the Butchers' Church because it was near to the Shambles. York's first fire engine was housed in the west chapel, which was known as Langton's Chantry. The headless ghost of Thomas Percy, executed for treason, is said to wander this dark quiet church.

**Holy Trinity Church, Goodramgate 1909** 61857

### ▼ St Olave's Church, Marygate c1885 18480

During the siege of York it is thought that guns were placed on the roof here, but there is some controversy about this. In about 1720 St Olave's was almost entirely rebuilt with stone from St Mary's Abbey. Adjacent to the church there was once a chapel called St-Mary-at-the-Gate, of which a small portion of the stonework still survives.

### St Mary's Abbey ▶ c1873 6619

Over time, much of the stone from this once very wealthy abbey was used on other buildings. The remaining ruins stand in Museum Gardens. It is said that the ghost of Anne Boleyn, who once stayed here, has been seen, and that the terrible cries of the dying that were placed in the courtyard after an attack by the Roundheads in 1644 can still be heard.

### ▲ The Minster c1890
Y12501

The south face was undergoing repair work at this time. Pollution, mainly from the smoke from the railways, did a lot of damage to both glass and stone. Between 1829 to 1984, there were three fires; the first was caused deliberately, the second was caused by a careless workman, and the third by lightning. All three caused terrible damage and loss, but we may be thankful that major restoration work was carried out.

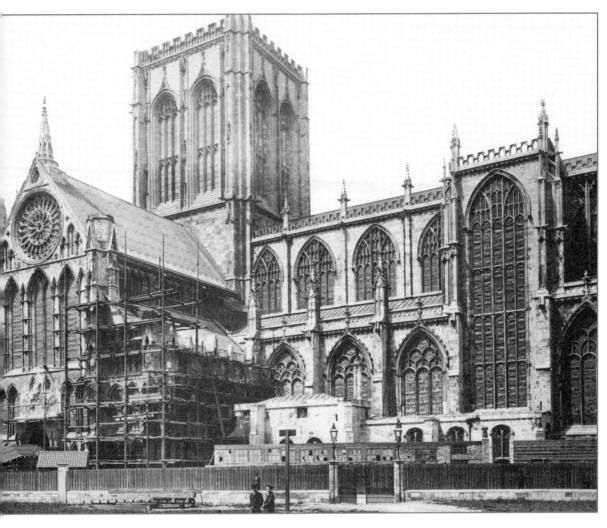

**The Minster 1897** 39491
There has been very little change to the appearance of this magnificent structure owing to careful restoration and repair, but the surroundings of the Minster have altered. On the grass to the left a statue of Constantine the Great, the Roman Emperor in 306, has been erected, and the roads are now much closer and almost surround the building.

◄ **The Minster, Choir East 1921** 70640
Here we can see the huge size of the magnificent stained glass window above the high altar. Made in the 13th century, it is larger than a tennis court. Releading of the window was begun when it was removed during the second world war for safety; the mammoth task took ten years to complete.

### ◀ The Minster 1908

59785

To the right of this view is Duncombe Place, with the tall memorial to the soldiers who took part in the Boer War. It was erected in 1905. One of the six statues that encircled it is now missing because lightning struck the memorial. The cross that crowned the memorial has also gone.

### ▼ Walmgate Bar c1885

18448

This view looks south-east. This is the only one of the four bars that has retained its barbican, or outer gateway. In 1793 John Browne, historian and artist of the Minster, was born in the timber-framed house on the inner side of the bar; it was still used as living accommodation up until 1959.

### ◀ Walmgate Bar c1955

Y12050

Walmgate has been burned and bombarded with cannon fire, and there was an attempt to undermine it using gunpowder during the siege of York in 1644. The mine has caused the ground to subside over time, which is probably the cause of the sagging in the side walls that is still visible. It was partially rebuilt after the siege, and completed in 1648 - this is recorded over the outer arch.

**Micklegate Bar c1885**  18440
This was the gateway that led to the road to London. In the 10th century, when
permission was granted for a house to be built on the bar, the yearly rent charged was
sixpence. Eventually Micklegate commanded the highest rent of the four bars: just over
13s. The walls of the passage are built with Roman stone, including used coffins.

**Micklegate Bar 1886** 18439
The heads of traitors and conspirators were often displayed on pikes here up until 1754, when the government called a halt to this practice because two of the heads were stolen by a Jacobite tailor. He was caught and fined £5 and sentenced to two years in jail. There are stories of ghosts frequenting the bar, including a gentleman dressed in black.

**Bootham Bar 1886** 18443
This, the northern gate, stands on the site of the Roman Porta Principalis, the gateway of Eboracum. The barbican was demolished in 1835. The name Bootham derives from Buthum, 'at the booths'; this probably related to market stalls that were set up nearby. The medieval statues that can just be seen on the top of the bar are in very poor condition and are hardly recognisable as figures.

**Bootham Bar and the Minster 1893** 32032
The stone-arched building on the right was the postern tower built in 1497 on St Mary's Abbey walls; it is now an office for First York Buses. The little cabmen's shelter at the side of the bar is no longer there. To the rear right of the bar we can see the turret on the roof of the Minster Chapter House.

**Bootham Bar 1909** 61701
The archway to this bar dates from the 11th century; this is the oldest of York's gates. In medieval times, guards were posted to keep watch and to guide people from the nearby Forest of Galtres so as to protect them from the packs of wolves that roamed the area.

**Bootham Bar 1911** 63585
Carved in 1894 by George Milburn, the statues on the top of the bar replaced the older, worn statues. The figures that now look down are Nicholas Langton, a Lord Mayor, a mason holding a model of the bar and a medieval knight. The coats of arms are the Stuart Royal Arms and the City Arms; these were renewed in 1969.

**Bootham Bar c1950** Y12008
The public house on the right is the White Horse; the statue of a horse can be seen rearing above the Tower Ales sign. Towards the bar old stonework still remains, with a sign for Pullman's Coaches. To the left, the corner shop with the large awning is now a bookmakers. These once quiet roads are now filled with heavy traffic.

**Bootham Bar c1955** Y12031
This view is taken from St Leonard's Place. The De Grey Rooms to the right were built in about 1841. The building was once used by the Yorkshire Hussars as an officers' mess; it is now the York Tourist Information Centre. The bus is heading for Linton, a scenic village in the Yorkshire Dales.

**Monk Bar c1885** 18442
With four storeys and standing at sixty-three feet high, this is the tallest of the four main bars, and also the most fortified - it was a self-contained fortress. As with all the bars, the rooms have had many different uses, including being used as a prison in the 16th century.

**Monk Bar c1950** Y12019
All four bars still have their portcullises, but this is the only one that still works. The statues on the parapet are holding rocks or boulders, and are ready to throw them at any invader. The origin of the small balcony is unknown, but public proclamations were read from there in the 17th century.

# The Rivers, the Bridges and the Views

The York of today probably would not exist if it was not for its geographical situation by the rivers. They were used to begin with to help form defences against attack and to monitor visitors, and then as a way to fetch and carry cargo of all kinds, from food to gunpowder.

The River Ouse flows in a south-easterly direction towards York, fed by the River Kyle and the River Nidd. The British East Coast main railway line crosses the Ouse just outside the city. Another railway bridge is used by the Scarborough to York line; it is a cast iron structure built in the mid ▶

**Naburn, The River c1955** N72012
Naburn is situated four miles south of York. In 1757 a weir and a lock were built to accommodate the river traffic. Once the water could hardly be seen for the many barges packing the river from bank to bank, carrying their vast variety of cargo from Hull to York.

19th century. When York's first railway station was constructed in 1840, it became necessary to build a crossing over the river for the extra traffic. Before this, the main means of getting from one side to the other was by ferry from Lendal crossing. The site chosen for the new bridge was where the ferry crossed. The building of the bridge began in 1860, but the structure collapsed a year into the construction, killing five men. Work began again, and Lendal Bridge was completed in 1863.

The present Ouse Bridge is at least the third and possibly the fourth that has spanned the river on or close to its present location. Because this was the only river crossing at the time, the bridge that stands now was built in two halves: the first part opened in 1818, and the other half of the old bridge was then demolished and the second half of the new bridge was completed. Skeldergate Bridge is the newest of the three. It opened in 1881, and was built to take the overload of the southern traffic that was using Ouse Bridge.

In 1068 the River Foss was dammed to provide water for the castle moat. This formed a large shallow lake known as the King's Fishpool (the fishing rights belonged exclusively to the king). This act had disastrous consequences, as it flooded well over 1,000 acres of arable land and destroyed many valuable buildings. Eventually in the mid 19th century the lake was drained - by then it had become stagnant.

Lining the riverbanks are many buildings and structures with a wealth of history that brings visitors flocking to see them. The rivers themselves are a playground for pleasure boats, and the bridges now carry much heavier and a different sort of traffic to when they were first built. Views over the older parts of the city can be seen by walking around the ancient walls. There are no skyscrapers or high-rise flats, so the one common factor in these views is York Minster, whose towers and spires can be seen rising above every building from many different vantage points.

**York Castle, Fishergate Postern c1885** 18496
The forbidding walls that surround the castle can be seen in the background. Originally there were six postern towers; the one at Fishergate is now the only one that remains unaltered. It once overlooked the King's Fishpool. On the first floor there was a lavatory that projected out over the lake.

**View from Skeldergate Bridge c1885** 18464
We are looking towards Ouse Bridge with South Esplanade on the right. The view has remained virtually the same, except for the difference in the river traffic and a change of use for some of the buildings. There are still private houses here, while others are now restaurants and bed and breakfasts catering for the many visitors.

◀ **Ouse Bridge 1885**
18463
Built in the 12th century, the original bridge was of wood and was probably sited nearer the Guildhall. Shops and houses, perhaps as many as fifty, were built on it. In 1565 the bridge collapsed. The new structure was rebuilt in stone later in the 16th century. The present bridge was built in the early 19th century.

### Skeldergate Bridge c1885 18457

The little castle-like building on the right of the bridge still remains. It was the toll house, and until 1914 it cost a halfpenny to cross. Opposite, in St George's Field, was the ducking stool used for scoundrels and females who served false measures or brewed bad beer.

### ▼ Ouse Bridge c1950
Y12005

The story is told (which may or may not be true) that in 1154 thousands of people lined the old bridge to herald the arrival of Archbishop William Fitzherbert, later to become St William of York. The weight of the crowds caused the bridge to collapse, but no-one was killed; because there was no loss of life, it was proclaimed a miracle.

### ◄ St Mary's Tower c1885 18455

This was the water tower for St Mary's Abbey. At one time the abbey boundary wall stood along the river bank. The little building to the rear, which here has 'baths' written on it, is now used as a store for canoes. The cart horses and their owners are waiting patiently to unload cargo from the moored boat - was it fish, perhaps?

◀ **Lendal Bridge 1909**
61702
The bridge was built in 1863 to replace the ferries that had been used to cross the river since the Middle Ages. The shields on either side depict the arms of the Diocese of York. A civic fountain was placed on the bridge in 1880 from which pets as well as people could drink. St Martin's Church tower can be seen behind the bridge.

### Lendal Tower c1885
18456

This tower was once linked by a chain to Barker's Tower on the opposite side of the river to stop craft entering the city without paying a tax. From the 17th century it was a pumping house for the town's water supply - the wheel was turned by horses. Nearby we can see the York Water Works Offices.

### ▼ The River c1950  Y12021

In this later view, we can see the Guildhall on the left side of the riverbank. As well as an underground passage opening right onto the water's edge, the Guildhall has two secret rooms. By the time of this photograph, the river was being used more and more for pleasure: streamlined boats are moored by the bank, and a canoe with its lone occupant is heading towards Lendal Bridge.

### ◄ The Castle from Castle Mill Bridge 1885  18494

The first recorded wooden bridge was built in 1583, and was destroyed during the siege of York. Two more were built after one another; the second was washed away by floods. This photograph, showing the castle walls and the dome of the Debtors' Prison, was taken from the fourth recorded bridge, which was replaced by the present one in 1955 owing to the demands of traffic.

**York Castle c1885**
18489
This wonderful view from the walls was taken before the onslaught of the motor car, and when gas lamps were still in place. As we look east over Skeldergate Bridge and the River Ouse to the left we can see the Assize Court; to the centre, standing out against the skyline is the spire of what was the Debtors' Prison and is now the Castle Museum.

**View from the Station Hotel c1885** 18432
This panoramic view takes in Lendal Tower, the Assize Court and the towers of the Minster in the distance. Outside the walls along the section near the hotel and station was a burial ground. Many of the victims of the cholera epidemic of 1832 were laid to rest there.

**View from the City Walls 1897** 39492
This and the following three photos, although from the same vantage point, span a period of 60 years. They show many changes in some of the buildings and in the mode of transport. Two horse-drawn vehicles can be seen on the road, and some people in their finery, the ladies twirling parasols, are on foot. Perhaps it is a Sunday and they are heading for church.

**View from the City Walls 1921** 70637
To the right of the view, the tall building, built in 1884, was
Walker's Repository for Horses; later, the building was shortened to
about half its height. A lone tram trundles around the corner, and a
few cars can be seen. To the rear of the photograph, on the right
of the Minster, stands the smaller tower of St Wilfred's Church,
which was built in 1864 and still stands.

**View from the City Walls c1940** Y12010
It is nearly 20 years later, and the area to the right is now completely built up. On the left, where the road sweeps round the corner, is the toll house for Lendal Bridge, built in 1863; it is now used as a teashop. The tram lines are plainly visible. Cars were still an unaffordable item to many, as we can see here from the almost empty roads.

**View from the City Walls c1955** Y12074
There have been many more changes to the buildings on the right, and now the tram lines have been removed; road markings, showing a one-way system, have taken their place. Cars and a bus form a queue heading for the city centre. The flower bed depicts the logo for the York Festival.

# Historical Buildings

Although there is not much of a distance between most of the buildings that are open to the public, plenty of time is needed to see them all. Each and every one has its own individuality and a different historical story to tell. A full day could easily be spent in the Castle Museum, which houses, besides many other attractions, a very interestingly-displayed collection of bygones. This term was coined by a young doctor, John Kirk from Pickering, in the early part of the 20th century. He felt that many everyday things were disappearing, often being thrown away because of more modern replacements, so he started a collection of discarded country objects, and included everything from furniture to kitchen utensils. Wishing his collection to be displayed, he approached many towns and cities in the area, but no-one was interested until Alderman J Morrell in York backed his idea. The old female prison was turned into the Kirk Museum. It became an instant success, and has remained a huge attraction. ▶

**Bishopthorpe Palace Gate c1885**  18499
The palace was built by the 33rd Archbishop of York, Walter de Gray, in about 1250, using stone from a previous manor house that he had had demolished. There is a large amount of wonderful medieval stained glass in the building, including the shields of nineteen of the past archbishops in the dining room.

Clifford's Tower, probably named for Roger de Clifford whose body was hung from the tower in chains in 1322, was twice built in timber and then rebuilt in stone. Because of the moat surrounding the tower, there were problems with subsidence; eventually it cracked in two places from top to bottom. For over one hundred years, from about 1825, it was included in the grounds of the prison, and a high wall surrounded both the tower and the prison buildings with no access to the public. It is now cared for by English Heritage.

The Mansion House is richly furnished, and boasts a wonderful collection of antique silver plate. While not open to the general public, an appointment can be made to visit the house at the Lord Mayor's discretion. Inside the Multiangular Tower, several stone Roman coffins that have been collected from different sites around the city can be seen. The Treasurer's House was in a state of disrepair when an industrialist, Frank Green, bought it in 1897 and restored the building. When he died in 1930, he left the house and its furniture to the National Trust. An exhibition is held in the basement on the life of the house since Roman times.

All kinds of buildings too numerous to mention individually (ancient towers that are now art galleries, small museums or craft centres, public houses, one dating from the 17th century, small timber-framed houses and lavishly elegant larger houses) jostle with each other for attention and show glimpses of a past that was both violent and bloody, prosperous and tasteful. York's past produced creativity and unbelievable workmanship that has left a legacy for all time.

**Bishopthorpe Palace from the Drive 1893** 32045
Extensions were added to the palace over the following century after it was first built. Then in 1647 Bishopthorpe was sold to a Colonel White, who added further to the building. During the Restoration the palace reverted to the church, and the great hall was rebuilt. Later, stables and another extension on the west side were added.

**Bishopthorpe Palace from the River 1893** 32044
A reflection in the river gives us a reflection of the past. This tranquil scene shows the many different styles of building that took place over more than six centuries to give this magnificent house its unique character.

**Bishopthorpe Palace Gardens 1893** 32047
Originally the village was known as Thorpe St Andrew; the name was changed to Bishopthorpe because of the archbishop's palace being built here. One can imagine the bishops using these peaceful gardens for prayer and meditation.

▼ **Heslington Hall c1960** Y12082
This elegant Elizabethan mansion was originally built for the Secretary
of the Council of the North in 1568. The hall changed hands many
times over the following centuries before being almost rebuilt in the
mid 19th century. The university became established here in 1963; it
now has a total of more than 3,000 students.

▼ **Heslington Hall, The University of York c1960** Y12080
This, the main body of the university, is spread over approximately 190
acres. The university uses many of the historical buildings in the city,
as well as the Hall. The statue, the Goddess Diana, was removed after
being damaged during student unrest in the 1970s.

▲ **The Infantry Barracks,
The Armoury 1886**
18705
York was a military
centre, and over 1,000
men were stationed here
when the barracks were
built. They had their own
hospital and a soldiers'
institute. Tower Street
housed the armoury for
the West Yorkshire
Volunteer Artillery, and
the York Volunteer Rifles
were in St Andrewgate.
The soldiers' superior
officer has let them stand
at ease for the camera!

◀ **The Infantry Barracks
The Armoury 1886** 18710
Situated on Fulford Road,
the barracks were originally
built around 1795 for the
14th Regimental District
and the West Yorkshire
Regiment. In 1951, to
commemorate exploits
in India, the site became
known as the Imphal
Barracks. The large keep on
view here is still in use.
A 25-pounder gun and a
Saladin armoured car are
preserved on the site.

◀ **The Cavalry Barracks, Main Guard 1886** 18719
These barracks were built about three years after the Infantry Barracks, but the construction came under much criticism. There were no litter sheds, and horse manure was piled up under the men's room windows. Also, there were no proper urinals for the men to use at night. Not an attraction for new recruits! Thank goodness, these problems were eventually sorted out.

### ◄ The Cavalry Barracks
### The Church 1886 18720

Gone from here are the men, horses, buildings and stables of the Royal Dragoon Guards. The site is now the Divisional Headquarters of the North Yorkshire Police. Only the church, which was known as the Garrison Church, remains, and it is now used by the police for storage. The other buildings were all demolished in the 1960s.

### ▼ The Cavalry Barracks
### 1886 18716

Watched over by their officers, the Royal Dragoons practice combat exercises using their swords. The regimental museum in Tower Street has displays of medals, uniforms and weapons, and models showing the battles that both this and other Yorkshire regiments fought in many parts of the world, including Egypt, Europe and the North-West Frontier.

### ◄ The War Office c1885
18468

The smart uniformed soldier stands silent guard outside this building, built in 1878 on the corner of Fishergate and Melbourne Street. It is still used for offices, but no longer by the War Department. A horse must have recently passed by, as it has left a deposit on the side of the road.

**The Law Courts 1893** 32039
This is now the Magistrates' Court, and it stands on the corner of Friargate and Clifford Street. It
is a rather dark, forbidding-looking structure, perhaps built that way to intimidate wrong-doers!
Next door, on the extreme left, the older building has now gone; the site is now occupied by
a modern one-storey fire station, which looks incongruous beside its large old neighbour.

**The Castle Gate c1885** 18492
These awe-inspiring and formidable walls and gates were knocked down in the 1920s. At that time there were no conservation laws, and anything that was in the way of progress was destroyed. The walls once surrounded both the castle and Clifford's Tower. The site of the old gate is now a car park.

**York Castle, Assize Court c1885** 18497
This was built in the 1770s; many notorious criminals were tried in York, including Dick Turpin in 1739. The area is known as the Eye of Yorkshire, or the Eye of the Ridings. Parliamentary elections were held here until the 19th century. Two of the courts are still used on a daily basis.

▼ **York Castle, the Old Prison, Dick Turpin's Cell c1885** 18493
When Dick Turpin was arrested and tried it was for horse stealing,
although his crimes included robbery and murder. He was using the
name of Palmer, and it was not until he was imprisoned that his true
identity was discovered. He was taken from the prison and hung at
Tyburn gallows at Knavesmire, now the site of the York Racetrack.

▼ **The Castle Museum c1955** Y12037
The land was acquired by the City Corporation in 1934 at a cost of £8,000. The
Debtors' Prison was opened as a museum, which was then extended to the
Women's Prison building. Amongst many other attractions, the museum has a
reconstruction of a Victorian shopping street. Thousands of people flock here
annually to this, one of the best-known museums in Britain.

▲ **Clifford's Tower 1885**
18488
Panoramic views of the
city can be seen from the
top of this tower, which
was built in the 12th
century to replace a
previous wooden castle.
The arms that can be
seen on the gatehouse
are of Henry Clifford, Earl
of Cumberland. Above
the gatehouse there is
a chapel.

### ◀ Clifford's Tower c1950
Y12018

Built on a motte which is about 48 feet high, the tower itself is just over 33 feet high. In the 16th century Robert Redhead, a gaoler, wanted to demolish the tower, but the people of York and the Corporation decided it should be kept as a treasure second only to the Minster.

**The Merchant Adventurers' Hall 1892** 30635
The hall was founded as a religious institution in 1357, and eventually came into the hands of the most powerful and wealthy traders in York. There is a chapel, portraits of past governors and many colourful banners in the building, which is now open to the public.

**The Merchant Adventurers' Hall 1909** 61851
Viewed here from the Fossgate entrance, the hall is the largest
timber-framed building in York; the undercroft is the oldest part.
The chapel, which was rebuilt in 1411, still retains part of the
original 15th-century oak screen and a 17th-century pulpit.

**A Tudor House c1950** Y12011
This house stands on the corner of Coney Street and New Street. The lower part of the house is now a shop that sells mobile telephones, but the upper storey remains virtually unchanged. The sign on the building to the right forefront of the photo advertises Stroud's Agency for Servants; it is now a fashion accessory shop. On the opposite side of the street, what was once a bank is now the Starbucks Coffee Shop.

**The Station Hotel c1885**  18434
This is the second Station Hotel; it was completed in 1878. Renamed the Royal York Hotel when it was bought in 1983, it is a Grade 2 listed building. The station and hotel were designed by Thomas Prosser. Both thrive to the present day. The first hotel, built about 1851, still stands to the east of the old railway station, and is used by British Rail as offices.

**The Station and the Hotel 1907**  58687
The new station was built to replace the original station that had been completed in 1841. Construction took place between 1873 and 1877 on the site of a Roman cemetery. When it was completed, it was said to be the largest station in the world. Here, to the left, the roof top can be seen; inside it sweeps in a wonderful curve above the main platforms.

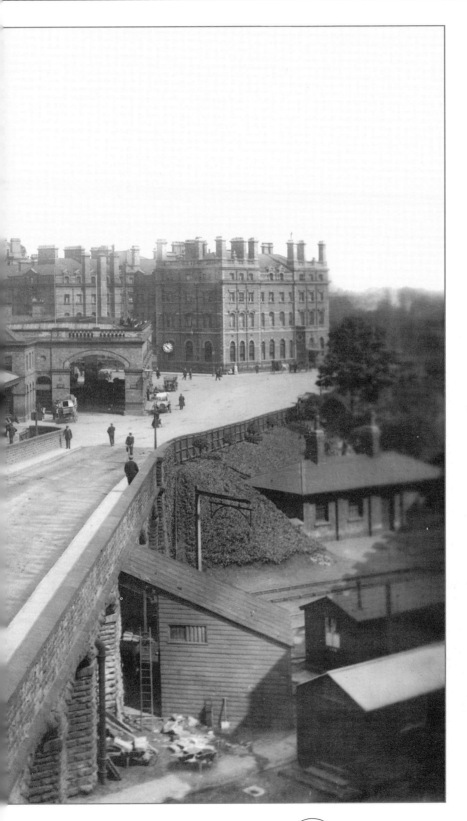

**The Station and the Hotel 1909** 61849
When the second station was constructed, new openings had to be made in the walls to give better access, because it was just outside the city walls. Much of the street plan was changed. One example was that Thieves Lane became Station Road.

◀ **The Volunteer War Monument 1909** 61719 This view shows the rear of the Assize Court. The whole area has changed almost beyond recognition. The castle walls to the right of the view are now demolished. The cannon is no longer there, and the monument, although still in almost the same place, now stands in the middle of a roundabout on a busy road.

### ◄ The North-Eastern Offices 1907  58689

This is the headquarters of British Rail Eastern Region, situated in Station Road. When this photograph was taken, the building had just been completed. Many different architectural styles were used, including Dutch gables. The badges on the building are of three different railway networks.

### ▼ The Guildhall c1885

18461

Over the centuries, the hall had been attacked by death watch beetle. Repairs began, but when in 1942 they were almost complete, the hall was bombed and very badly damaged. In the 1950s the hall was rebuilt as near to the original design as possible. Each of the pillars in the main hall are from a single oak tree donated by the county families of Yorkshire.

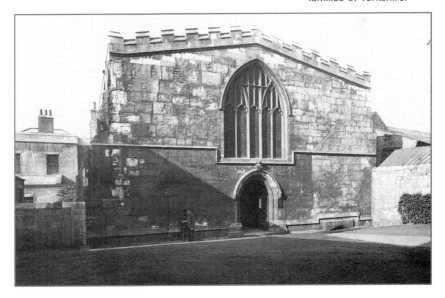

### ◄ The Mansion House c1955  Y12048

In St Helen's Square, what had been a Guildhall Chapel and then a public house was demolished to make way for the building of a residence for the Lord Mayor. The result was this charming abode. It was built in about 1775, and is now one of the three oldest surviving buildings of its kind in England.

### ▼ The Multiangular Tower c1885  18485

The lower part of this strange structure is Roman; it was the west corner of the Roman fort. The upper part is 14th-century. Inside, there is a small ruined tower. When this stretch of the wall was excavated, the archaeologists found that the ramparts dated from Roman, Saxon, Viking, Norman and medieval times, and that the earth bank grew with each occupation.

### ▼ The Hospitium c1885  18483

Near the River Ouse, situated in what is now the Museum Gardens, this building was the guest house for St Mary's Abbey. The ground floor was built in the early 14th century, while the timber-framed first floor was added in 1420; a new roof was built in the 1930s.

### ▲ The Ancient Palace of the Stuart Kings 1909

61720

Built around 1280 for the Abbot of St Mary's Abbey, the building was enlarged in the 15th century. Although belonging to the King, and known as the King's Manor, it was never used as a royal residence. It is now owned by the University of York, and parts are open to the public, including the impressive Huntingdon Room built by the Earl of Huntingdon.

### ◄ The Exhibition c1885

18466

An exhibition of fine art was held in the grounds of Bootham Park Hospital in 1866. It attracted thousands of people, so it was decided that a permanent building for further exhibitions should be erected. This building, in what became known as Exhibition Square, opened in 1879; it is now the York City Art Gallery.

**The Treasurer's House 1908** 59796
In this, the most interesting of all the houses in York, a young apprentice plumber stated that while he was working in the cellar, he heard a trumpet playing; then he saw an army of Roman soldiers marching, but as if on their knees. When the cellar floor was dug up, the remains of a Roman road was discovered where the soldiers' feet would have been!

**St William's College 1892** 30634
The college was first built for the Minster's Chantry Priests in about 1465. These priests had plenty of money and plenty of time on their hands, and were always getting up to mischief. It was decided to house them somewhere so that they could be close to the Minster, but out of the way of trouble.

**St William's College 1908** 59795
When Charles I moved with his court to York, the royal printing press was housed here. Over the years, many owners and many changes of use left the building in a ramshackle state. In fact, it was so dilapidated that at one point there were plans to demolish it, but it was saved and restored.

**St William's College 1920** 69602
Photograph No 61852 shows neglect, but now, a few years later, there have been improvements. The interior quadrangular courtyard is entered from College Street through an arched gateway. Above the entrance is a stone figure of St William (the Archbishop of York) who died in 1154. Nowadays the courtyard is well-cared-for.

◄ **St William's College**
**1909** 61852
The building was named after William Fitzherbert, who was the great-grandson of William the Conqueror. At the turn of the 19th century, the building was used as tenements. The Convocation of York eventually bought the property; they used it as a meeting place until the amalgamation with the Church of England.

▼ **St William's College**
**1911** 63600
This view shows clearly the entrance to the courtyard in the centre of the building. The exterior is part of the original 15th-century structure, and must look very much the same as when it was first built. The interior, however, is mainly of the 17th and 18th centuries, owing to the different owners in various periods of time.

◄ **St William's College, The Layman's Room**
**1911** 63606
Two brothers who rented rooms here robbed and murdered a cleric. The younger brother hid in a chest with the booty, but was found and hung after his older brother gave him away. The older brother, although free, was haunted by guilt and died quite young. It is said that his footsteps can still be heard at night pacing the upper floors.

◀ **St William's College
c1950** Y12014
The central doors, which
can just be seen in this
photograph, were made
by the famous wood
carver, Thompson of
Kilburn: his signature,
a mouse, is carved on
the right-hand door. The
College is now open to
the public as a restaurant
and exhibition hall.

◀ **The Minster, the East End and St William's College 1913** 65443
As we can see, it was just a hop and a skip for the chantry priests to reach the Minster from their dwellings. At the time of this scene, the building would have been tenements. The children on the steps seem fascinated by the photographer.

▼ **Clifton, St Peter's School 1909** 61724
The original building was built as a small private school in 1838. In 1844 it was acquired by the Dean and Chapter to use for St Peter's School, which had outgrown its former site. It is now the oldest public school in England. The architecture of the building is mainly Gothic revival.

◀ **The County Hospital 1913** 65463
The hospital was founded in 1749 and rebuilt in 1850. This building eventually closed as a hospital and became offices for the water board. For the last few years it has been used as flats. The area to the right is now a Sainsbury's supermarket. Here the gardener can be seen having a respite from his toil to stand and watch the photographer.

# Snickelways and Streets

Some of the old streets have disappeared altogether, or have been incorporated into other streets to house the office blocks and shopping developments - or just to make more room for the heavy traffic that all towns and cities have to contend with. However, we may be thankful that many of the medieval streets survive, giving an insight on the layout of York before the motor car and the tourist. Ginnels, narrow twisting alleys, snickelways and little cobbled streets curve and wind around each other, all with their separate purposes. Some lead to the most unexpected surprises - perhaps a pretty courtyard belonging to a private house, bedecked with hanging baskets. Many of these little alleys were short cuts to markets; although they have survived as rights of way, they have been built around and sometimes over. The facing houses often lean towards each other, and one can imagine the women shouting over

**Coney Street 1909**  61723
In the 1920s, the owner of a chain of grocery stores had two carved cats placed on the upper front of his shop - they were supposed to frighten the rats away from the river bank. The large clock on its ornamental bracket outside St Martin's Church dates from 1668; it still shows present-day shoppers the time. The chap in the smart motor car looks a proper toff!

the streets from their upstairs windows to their neighbours opposite. One of the drawbacks would have been the filth littering the streets; women would have to lift their skirts and petticoats high to stop them trailing in the dirt. Often the shop fronts would have been open, like market stalls, allowing the sellers to display their wares to the public. Many carvings survive on the houses and shop fronts. Some had superstitious significance - they warded off bad luck or brought good luck. Others were just for decorative purposes, or to advertise a particular shop or trade. A statue of Minerva, the goddess of wisdom, sits with her arm leaning on a pile of books looking down from the corner of Minster Gates, which was once known as Bookbinder's Alley. In Coney Street, standing on the top of the clock of St Martin's Church is 'the little admiral', a naval officer looking through a sextant.

Names in York are rather confusing. Bar derives from 'gata' or gate, gate means street, a yard is an alley and a court is a yard. The shortest street in the city has the longest name, Whip-Ma-Whop-Ma-Gate. Coppergate was the street of coopers, Stonegate was full of bookshops. One of the carvings that still remains here is a red chained devil on the corner of Coffee Yard above the shop front of No 33. Boys that fetched and carried the type for the printers were called printer's devils. The first known press was in Stonegate in 1509, and the first newspaper in York was printed here in 1719. Other less-well-known names, but old and quaint ones, are Pope's Head Alley and Mad Alice Lane - this was named after Alice Smith, who was hung for insanity.

Now the shop fronts have been modernised, and gone are the open benches where wares were displayed and the later square panes of the Georgian windows. The shops are now full of fashion accessories, gifts and antiques, but above the shops many of the second storeys of the buildings still retain the features of their period.

**Stonegate 1886**  18449
The boy dressed in breeches with cap in hand looks a little lost soul standing in the almost empty cobbled street.
On the left there is a sign for Waddingtons Piano Forte Manufacturers. The street banner advertises Boddy's Star
Inn, which was No 40 on the right of the view. Mr Boddy was the proprietor until 1894, when he died at the inn.

**Stonegate c1960** Y12055
Here the wording on the banner has been changed to 'Ye Olde Starre Inne'. Once there would have been many of these gallows signs, as they are called, but this is the only one remaining in York. Sometimes the signs would hang so low that people would have to duck to pass by. The 17th-century inn has survived, but it has been totally altered.

**The Market 1908** 59799
This crowded scene shows the stalls sited on Parliament Street in St Sampson's Square. The market was moved to nearby Newgate in 1955. At the forefront to the left of the photograph is a horse-drawn bus with baskets of wares being carried on the roof. The age of the motor car was just dawning.

**The Shambles 1909** 61722
The children pictured here have been captured forever in their innocence, looking at the photographer from a very
dilapidated-looking Shambles. The shops appear to be deserted, with even a door removed from its hinges. The
street looks very different nowadays, with the hustle and bustle of visitors sightseeing and shopping.

**The Shambles c1960** Y12071
The word Shambles derives from 'shamel', meaning benches or stalls. In the 15th century, this little street was full of open-fronted butchers' stalls with the meat being displayed hanging from large hooks. Up to the 19th century there were still many butchers selling their meat here.

**The Shambles c1962** Y12062
The Shambles was originally known as Haymongergate, because it was the site of the haymarket. Hay was used to feed the animals awaiting slaughter; it was illegal to graze livestock within six miles of the city centre. The street is very narrow, and at one point outstretched hands can touch each other from the opposite sides of the upper storeys.

**Little Shambles Market c1960** Y12063
The wealthy Butchers' Guild once had a guildhall in this street; it was demolished in the 19th century. At the Pavement end of the street stood the town pillory - anyone found guilty of treason was beheaded here. Little Shambles is called so because it is only a few yards in length.

**Low Petergate 1892**
30632
On the right is
Merriman's
Pawnbrokers, with its
leaf-decorated lamp
hanging above the shop
front. On the left is a
large sweeping brush
head trade sign, now in
the York Castle
Museum: it advertised
Seale's Brush and Mat
Warehouse. The lamp
to the forefront on the
Londesbro Arms has
now disappeared.

**Low Petergate c1950** Y12006
In this view, Seales Warehouse is now a toy shop, and next door is York's Pram and Nursery Furniture Centre. On the right is the Fox Inn, which still remains. Perhaps the two gentlemen talking outside Merrimans have something to pawn!

**Low Petergate c1960** Y12061
A carved wooden Indian holding a cigar still stands silent guard above one of the shop fronts in this street; it was once used to symbolise to the illiterate that the shop was a tobacconist. Scaffolding is in place on one of the Minster towers, as serious repairs were taking place.

**Low Petergate c1960** Y12060
This view was taken from King's Square. The street was originally part of the Roman city's main road, or Via Principalis. The pawnbroker has gone; instead there is a modern shopping block housing the furniture shop of Stevens and Goodall.

**Goodramgate 1886**
3443 To the left of the street is a gate, erected in 1766, which leads to Holy Trinity Church. The houses here, on what is called Our Lady's Row, are amongst the oldest in England - they are early 14th-century. To the right of this view is the Sanderson's Temperance Hotel, now long gone. Shops now line this side of the street.

**Goodramgate 1892**

30631

The covered way at the side of J Todd's Grocer and Tea Dealer was built for the vicars-choral, so that they could cross from where they lived in Bedern to the Minster Yard without being molested. The grocer's became an office for the National Trust in 1903. It was situated where College Street joins Goodramgate on the eastern side.

**College Street c1960** Y12053
Once known as Vicar's Lane and then Little Alice Lane, the street branches off to Minster Yard, where the Theatre Royal opened in 1730 - it was the first theatre in York. The road to the front of the houses is now much wider, and there is a small park opposite the college.

**Rawcliffe, The High Street c1955** R236004
The old model petrol pump looks rather incongruous standing in front of the house doorway. On the green, which consisted of nearly two acres of land, there was once a horse pond and a maypole; the horse pond was replaced with a drinking trough for cattle. The lady looks ready to pull down the sun awnings!

# Index

# Frith Book Co Titles

## www.frithbook.co.uk

The Frith Book Company publishes over 100 new titles each year. A selection of those currently available are listed below. For latest catalogue please contact Frith Book Co.

Town Books 96pp, 100 photos. County and Themed Books 128pp, 150 photos (unless specified). All titles hardback laminated case and jacket except those indicated pb (paperback)

| | | | | | | |
|---|---|---|---|---|---|---|
| Around Bakewell | 1-85937-113-2 | £12.99 | | Around Great Yarmouth | 1-85937-085-3 | £12.99 |
| Around Barnstaple | 1-85937-084-5 | £12.99 | | Around Guildford | 1-85937-117-5 | £12.99 |
| Around Bath | 1-85937-097-7 | £12.99 | | Hampshire | 1-85937-064-0 | £14.99 |
| Berkshire (pb) | 1-85937-191-4 | £9.99 | | Around Harrogate | 1-85937-112-4 | £12.99 |
| Around Blackpool | 1-85937-049-7 | £12.99 | | Around Horsham | 1-85937-127-2 | £12.99 |
| Around Bognor Regis | 1-85937-055-1 | £12.99 | | Around Ipswich | 1-85937-133-7 | £12.99 |
| Around Bournemouth | 1-85937-067-5 | £12.99 | | Ireland (pb) | 1-85937-181-7 | £9.99 |
| Brighton (pb) | 1-85937-192-2 | £8.99 | | Isle of Man | 1-85937-065-9 | £14.99 |
| British Life A Century Ago | 1-85937-103-5 | £17.99 | | Isle of Wight | 1-85937-114-0 | £14.99 |
| Buckinghamshire (pb) | 1-85937-200-7 | £9.99 | | Kent (pb) | 1-85937-189-2 | £9.99 |
| Around Cambridge | 1-85937-092-6 | £12.99 | | Around Leicester | 1-85937-073-x | £12.99 |
| Cambridgeshire | 1-85937-086-1 | £14.99 | | Leicestershire (pb) | 1-85937-185-x | £9.99 |
| Canals and Waterways | 1-85937-129-9 | £17.99 | | Around Lincoln | 1-85937-111-6 | £12.99 |
| Cheshire | 1-85937-045-4 | £14.99 | | Lincolnshire | 1-85937-135-3 | £14.99 |
| Around Chester | 1-85937-090-x | £12.99 | | London (pb) | 1-85937-183-3 | £9.99 |
| Around Chichester | 1-85937-089-6 | £12.99 | | Around Maidstone | 1-85937-056-x | £12.99 |
| Churches of Berkshire | 1-85937-170-1 | £17.99 | | New Forest | 1-85937-128-0 | £14.99 |
| Churches of Dorset | 1-85937-172-8 | £17.99 | | Around Newark | 1-85937-105-1 | £12.99 |
| Colchester (pb) | 1-85937-188-4 | £8.99 | | Around Newquay | 1-85937-140-x | £12.99 |
| Cornwall | 1-85937-054-3 | £14.99 | | North Devon Coast | 1-85937-146-9 | £14.99 |
| Cumbria | 1-85937-101-9 | £14.99 | | Northumberland and Tyne & Wear | | |
| Dartmoor | 1-85937-145-0 | £14.99 | | | 1-85937-072-1 | £14.99 |
| Around Derby | 1-85937-046-2 | £12.99 | | Norwich (pb) | 1-85937-194-9 | £8.99 |
| Derbyshire (pb) | 1-85937-196-5 | £9.99 | | Around Nottingham | 1-85937-060-8 | £12.99 |
| Devon | 1-85937-052-7 | £14.99 | | Nottinghamshire (pb) | 1-85937-187-6 | £9.99 |
| Dorset | 1-85937-075-6 | £14.99 | | Around Oxford | 1-85937-096-9 | £12.99 |
| Dorset Coast | 1-85937-062-4 | £14.99 | | Oxfordshire | 1-85937-076-4 | £14.99 |
| Down the Severn | 1-85937-118-3 | £14.99 | | Peak District | 1-85937-100-0 | £14.99 |
| Down the Thames | 1-85937-121-3 | £14.99 | | Around Penzance | 1-85937-069-1 | £12.99 |
| Around Dublin | 1-85937-058-6 | £12.99 | | Around Plymouth | 1-85937-119-1 | £12.99 |
| East Sussex | 1-85937-130-2 | £14.99 | | Around St Ives | 1-85937-068-3 | £12.99 |
| Around Eastbourne | 1-85937-061-6 | £12.99 | | Around Scarborough | 1-85937-104-3 | £12.99 |
| Edinburgh (pb) | 1-85937-193-0 | £8.99 | | Scotland (pb) | 1-85937-182-5 | £9.99 |
| English Castles | 1-85937-078-0 | £14.99 | | Scottish Castles | 1-85937-077-2 | £14.99 |
| Essex | 1-85937-082-9 | £14.99 | | Around Sevenoaks and Tonbridge | | |
| Around Exeter | 1-85937-126-4 | £12.99 | | | 1-85937-057-8 | £12.99 |
| Exmoor | 1-85937-132-9 | £14.99 | | Around Southampton | 1-85937-088-8 | £12.99 |
| Around Falmouth | 1-85937-066-7 | £12.99 | | Around Southport | 1-85937-106-x | £12.99 |

## Available from your local bookshop or from the publisher

# Frith Book Co Titles (continued)

| | | | | | | |
|---|---|---|---|---|---|---|
| Scottish Castles | 1-85937-077-2 | £14.99 | Around Torbay | 1-85937-063-2 | £12.99 |
| Around Sevenoaks and Tonbridge | 1-85937-057-8 | £12.99 | Around Truro | 1-85937-147-7 | £12.99 |
| Around Southampton | 1-85937-088-8 | £12.99 | Victorian & Edwardian Kent | 1-85937-149-3 | £14.99 |
| Around Southport | 1-85937-106-x | £12.99 | Victorian & Edwardian Maritime Album | | |
| Around Shrewsbury | 1-85937-110-8 | £12.99 | | 1-85937-144-2 | £17.99 |
| Shropshire | 1-85937-083-7 | £14.99 | Victorian & Edwardian Yorkshire | 1-85937-154-x | £14.99 |
| South Devon Coast | 1-85937-107-8 | £14.99 | Victorian Seaside | 1-85937-159-0 | £17.99 |
| South Devon Living Memories | 1-85937-168-x | £14.99 | Warwickshire (pb) | 1-85937-203-1 | £9.99 |
| Staffordshire (96pp) | 1-85937-047-0 | £12.99 | Welsh Castles | 1-85937-120-5 | £14.99 |
| Stone Circles & Ancient Monuments | | | West Midlands | 1-85937-109-4 | £14.99 |
| | 1-85937-143-4 | £17.99 | West Sussex | 1-85937-148-5 | £14.99 |
| Around Stratford upon Avon | 1-85937-098-5 | £12.99 | Wiltshire | 1-85937-053-5 | £14.99 |
| Sussex (pb) | 1-85937-184-1 | £9.99 | Around Winchester | 1-85937-139-6 | £12.99 |

# Frith Book Co titles available Autumn 2000

| | | | | | | | |
|---|---|---|---|---|---|---|---|
| Cotswolds (pb) | 1-85937-230-9 | £9.99 | Sep | English Country Houses | 1-85937-161-2 | £17.99 | Oct |
| Cornish Coast | 1-85937-163-9 | £14.99 | Sep | Folkestone (pb) | 1-85937-124-8 | £9.99 | Oct |
| County Durham | 1-85937-123-x | £14.99 | Sep | Humberside | 1-85937-215-5 | £14.99 | Oct |
| Dorset Living Memories | 1-85937-210-4 | £14.99 | Sep | Manchester (pb) | 1-85937-198-1 | £9.99 | Oct |
| Dublin (pb) | 1-85937-231-7 | £9.99 | Sep | Norfolk Living Memories | 1-85937-217-1 | £14.99 | Oct |
| Herefordshire | 1-85937-174-4 | £14.99 | Sep | Preston (pb) | 1-85937-212-0 | £9.99 | Oct |
| Kent Living Memories | 1-85937-125-6 | £14.99 | Sep | Reading (pb) | 1-85937-238-4 | £9.99 | Oct |
| Leeds (pb) | 1-85937-202-3 | £9.99 | Sep | Salisbury (pb) | 1-85937-239-2 | £9.99 | Oct |
| Ludlow (pb) | 1-85937-176-0 | £9.99 | Sep | South Hams | 1-85937-220-1 | £14.99 | Oct |
| Norfolk (pb) | 1-85937-195-7 | £9.99 | Sep | Suffolk (pb) | 1-85937-221-x | £9.99 | Oct |
| North Yorks (pb) | 1-85937-236-8 | £9.99 | Sep | Swansea (pb) | 1-85937-167-1 | £9.99 | Oct |
| Somerset | 1-85937-153-1 | £14.99 | Sep | West Yorkshire (pb) | 1-85937-201-5 | £9.99 | Oct |
| Surrey (pb) | 1-85937-240-6 | £9.99 | Sep | | | | |
| Tees Valley & Cleveland | 1-85937-211-2 | £14.99 | Sep | Around Aylesbury (pb) | 1-85937-227-9 | £9.99 | Nov |
| Thanet (pb) | 1-85937-116-7 | £9.99 | Sep | Around Bradford (pb) | 1-85937-204-x | £9.99 | Nov |
| Tiverton (pb) | 1-85937-178-7 | £9.99 | Sep | Around Chichester (pb) | 1-85937-228-7 | £9.99 | Nov |
| Victorian and Edwardian Sussex | | | | East Anglia (pb) | 1-85937-265-1 | £9.99 | Nov |
| | 1-85937-157-4 | £14.99 | Sep | East London | 1-85937-080-2 | £14.99 | Nov |
| Weymouth (pb) | 1-85937-209-0 | £9.99 | Sep | Gloucestershire | 1-85937-102-7 | £14.99 | Nov |
| Worcestershire | 1-85937-152-3 | £14.99 | Sep | Greater Manchester (pb) | 1-85937-266-x | £9.99 | Nov |
| Yorkshire Living Memories | 1-85937-166-3 | £14.99 | Sep | Hastings & Bexhill (pb) | 1-85937-131-0 | £9.99 | Nov |
| | | | | Helston (pb) | 1-85937-214-7 | £9.99 | Nov |
| British Life A Century Ago (pb) | | | | Lancaster, Morecombe & Heysham (pb) | | | |
| | 1-85937-213-9 | £9.99 | Oct | | 1-85937-233-3 | £9.99 | Nov |
| Camberley (pb) | 1-85937-222-8 | £9.99 | Oct | Peterborough (pb) | 1-85937-219-8 | £9.99 | Nov |
| Cardiff (pb) | 1-85937-093-4 | £9.99 | Oct | Piers | 1-85937-237-6 | £17.99 | Nov |
| Carmarthenshire | 1-85937-216-3 | £14.99 | Oct | Wiltshire Living Memories | 1-85937-245-7 | £14.99 | Nov |
| Cheltenham (pb) | 1-85937-095-0 | £9.99 | Oct | Windmills & Watermills | 1-85937-242-2 | £17.99 | Nov |
| Cornwall (pb) | 1-85937-229-5 | £9.99 | Oct | York (pb) | 1-85937-199-x | £9.99 | Nov |

## See Frith books on the internet www.frithbook.co.uk

# FRITH PRODUCTS & SERVICES

Francis Frith would doubtless be pleased to know that the pioneering publishing venture he started in 1860 still continues today. A hundred and forty years later, The Francis Frith Collection continues in the same innovative tradition and is now one of the foremost publishers of vintage photographs in the world. Some of the current activities include:

## Interior Decoration

Today Frith's photographs can be seen framed and as giant wall murals in thousands of pubs, restaurants, hotels, banks, retail stores and other public buildings throughout the country. In every case they enhance the unique local atmosphere of the places they depict and provide reminders of gentler days in an increasingly busy and frenetic world.

## Product Promotions

Frith products are used by many major companies to promote the sales of their own products or to reinforce their own history and heritage. Frith promotions have been used by Hovis bread, Courage beers, Scots Porage Oats, Colman's mustard, Cadbury's foods, Mellow Birds coffee, Dunhill pipe tobacco, Guinness, and Bulmer's Cider.

## Genealogy and Family History

As the interest in family history and roots grows world-wide, more and more people are turning to Frith's photographs of Great Britain for images of the towns, villages and streets where their ancestors lived; and, of course, photographs of the churches and chapels where their ancestors were christened, married and buried are an essential part of every genealogy tree and family album.

## Frith Products

All Frith photographs are available Framed or just as Mounted Prints and Posters (size 23 x 16 inches). These may be ordered from the address below. From time to time other products - Address Books, Calendars, Table Mats, etc - are available.

## The Internet

Already twenty thousand Frith photographs can be viewed and purchased on the internet. By the end of the year 2000 some 60,000 Frith photographs will be available on the internet. The number of sites is constantly expanding, each focussing on different products and services from the Collection.
The main Frith sites are listed below.
www.francisfrith.co.uk
www.frithbook.co.uk

---

**See the complete list of Frith Books at:**
*www.frithbook.co.uk*
This web site is regularly updated with the latest list of publications from the Frith Book Company. If you wish to buy books relating to another part of the country that your local bookshop does not stock, you may purchase on-line.

---

*For further information, trade, or author enquiries please contact us at the address below:*
**The Francis Frith Collection, Frith's Barn, Teffont, Salisbury, Wiltshire, England SP3 5QP.**
Tel: +44 (0)1722 716 376  Fax: +44 (0)1722 716 881  Email: uksales@francisfrith.co.uk

## See Frith books on the internet www.frithbook.co.uk

## TO RECEIVE YOUR FREE MOUNTED PRINT

**Mounted Print**
*Overall size 14 x 11 inches*

*Cut out this Voucher and return it with your remittance for £1.50 to cover postage and handling, to UK addresses. For overseas addresses please include £4.00 post and handling. Choose any photograph included in this book. Your SEPIA print will be A4 in size, and mounted in a cream mount with burgundy rule lines, overall size 14 x 11 inches.*

### Order additional Mounted Prints at HALF PRICE (only £7.49 each*)

If there are further pictures you would like to order, possibly as gifts for friends and family, purchase them at half price (no additional postage and handling required).

### Have your Mounted Prints framed*

For an additional £14.95 per print you can have your chosen Mounted Print framed in an elegant polished wood and gilt moulding, overall size 16 x 13 inches (no additional postage and handling required).

---

**\* IMPORTANT!**
**These special prices are only available if ordered using the original voucher on this page (no copies permitted) and at the same time as your free Mounted Print, for delivery to the same address**

---

## Frith Collectors' Guild

*From time to time we publish a magazine of news and stories about Frith photographs and further special offers of Frith products. If you would like 12 months FREE membership, please return this form.*

*Send completed forms to:*
**The Francis Frith Collection, Frith's Barn, Teffont, Salisbury, Wiltshire SP3 5QP**

---

# *Voucher* for **FREE** and Reduced Price Frith Prints

| Picture no. | Page number | Qty | Mounted @ £7.49 | Framed + £14.95 | Total Cost |
|---|---|---|---|---|---|
| | | 1 | Free of charge* | £ | £ |
| | | | £7.49 | £ | £ |
| | | | £7.49 | £ | £ |
| | | | £7.49 | £ | £ |
| | | | £7.49 | £ | £ |
| | | | £7.49 | £ | £ |

| | | |
|---|---|---|
| *Please allow 28 days for delivery* | **\* Post & handling** | **£1.50** |
| **Book Title** . . . . . . . . . . . . . . . | **Total Order Cost** | **£** |

*Please do not photocopy this voucher. Only the original is valid, so please cut it out and return it to us.*

I enclose a cheque / postal order for £ . . . . . . . . . . made payable to 'The Francis Frith Collection' OR please debit my Mastercard / Visa / Switch / Amex card *(credit cards please on all overseas orders)*

Number . . . . . . . . . . . . . . . . . . . . . . . . . . . . . .

Issue No(Switch only) . . . . . . . .Valid from (Amex/Switch) . . . . . . .

Expires . . . . . . . . . . Signature . . . . . . . . . . . . . . . .

Name Mr/Mrs/Ms . . . . . . . . . . . . . . . . . . . . . . . . . . . .

Address . . . . . . . . . . . . . . . . . . . . . . . . . . . . . . . . . .

. . . . . . . . . . . . . . . . . . . . . . . . . . . . . . . . . . . . . . . .

. . . . . . . . . . . . . . . . . . . . . . Postcode . . . . . . . . . . . . .

Daytime Tel No . . . . . . . . . . . . . . . . . . . .   Valid to 31/12/02

---

## The Francis Frith Collectors' Guild

Please enrol me as a member for 12 months free of charge.

Name Mr/Mrs/Ms . . . . . . . . . . . . . . . . . . . . . . . . . . . .

Address . . . . . . . . . . . . . . . . . . . . . . . . . . . . . . . . . .

. . . . . . . . . . . . . . . . . . . . . . . . . . . . . . . . . . . . . . . .

. . . . . . . . . . . . . . . . . . . . . . Postcode . . . . . . . . . . . . .

Free Print - see overleaf